staring at the animal

Tupelo Press Snowbound Series
Chapbook Award Winners

Barbara Tran, *In the Mynah Bird's Own Words*
Selected by Robert Wrigley

David Hernandez, *A House Waiting for Music*
Selected by Ray Gonzalez

Mark Yakich, *The Making of Collateral Beauty*
Selected by Mary Ruefle

Joy Katz, *The Garden Room*
Selected by Lisa Russ Spaar

Cecilia Woloch, *Narcissus*
Selected by Marie Howe

John Cross, *staring at the animal*
Selected by Gillian Conoley

staring at the animal

john cross

TUPELO PRESS
NORTH ADAMS, MASSACHUSETTS

Cover and text designed by Bill Kuch, WK Graphic Design.
Printed in the United States.
First paperback edition: November 2009.

Tupelo Press
P.O. Box 1767, North Adams, Massachusetts 01247
Telephone: (413) 664-9611 / Fax: (413) 664-9711
editor@tupelopress.org / www.tupelopress.org

Tupelo Press is an award-winning independent literary press that publishes
fine fiction, non-fiction, and poetry in books that are a joy to hold as well as
read. Tupelo Press is a registered 501(c)3 non-profit organization, and we
rely on public support to carry out our mission of publishing extraordinary
work that may be outside the realm of the large commercial publishers.
Financial donations are welcome and are tax deductible.

For Christine, without whom nothing would exist.

✑ Contents ✑

staring at the animal

heat

a good sun   pulls a picture from the wreckage
                finds subtle hollows in the metal
                          hair cuttings & butcher's twine

a good sun   flaps its r's outside the window
                raises high the ridges of rooftops
                          everything inside pushed to the corner furthest away

a good sun   feels for the saltwater of its handkerchief
                      for the peacock of its bonfire
                        the line where her lips meet

a good sun   notes the vacancy of the dental chair
                      the moon's plaster teeth snapping like neon
                      the palm of its white drum

a good sun   gathers leaves at night
                murmurs blankets of snow
                      faint light cusping the ghostweed

a good sun   when it hears what we've done
                pushes down on our feet

When Possible We Try to See

while you slept   [   ]   things too large

    to move through the house   did

*

under the kliegs

    they dug & they dug deeper   till they could find no more teeth

      & no shadow
      to delineate
      no blue-edged   forest

*

& we ran our fingers

    along the edges

      of our fractured bones

    learning to read:

*

wild prairie dog   wild prairie indigo

    wild prairie grass

    wild prairie muralist

*

while you slept   I pulled on a blue uniform

worked on drafts of unforgivable diagrams

                    with a triangle of knotted rope

three by four by five   measured it out

& we arrive

*

while you sleep   I wait at the bar

          [cigarette-jukebox-farm-town-haze

                    -rusty-railroad-haunted]

*

while you sleep   one neon graveyard

          as a moth does wool

                    ticking in the sun

quiet store

sometimes I feel like uprooting them, I'd like to tell you
sharpening their claws to scratch another's, belonging to another

leaves dazzle at the last minute, morning makes red
small & twisted notes, ones who disappear, ashamed

but on the inside is extremely loving for me
I tell her, "things occur to me, I'd like for someone

to slowly move away along the sidewalk, to explain to me
at the last minute, why I hear the quiet store, I hear emptying out

I hear breathing"

After Marey's First Mechanical Bird

o   dusk field   panicle of washerwomen
when the eye skerricks to frame   light's brief shudder
birds are a particular problem   each surge
                              brokenly language

and a northern raven *tokking* up the spine
of a winter maple   (closing of a hand)
wing shards cooked in a star   about to happen
                              first dazzling slivers

          descend   *descend*   out of the edgy god-light
you spangly nail studded   [missing]   black hangar
awned   plangent   drift
                              the disassembling glitters

Antigone Sequence

#(at Colonus)

: the Greek girl keeps pigeons over her father's tiny blue-screams
  it carry old swell-foot's pain

: between the cage's wire grates
  it young eat the head off it

: the Greek girl, eyes crowded, leaves her father. unqualitied, he handguesses
          the change
  old cane-tap scald it soft parts

: pushed-out little bluish knots of cry
  it eat the head off it young

: it don't quiet, forevered

:

early riser

getting rid clears my head
I fall asleep, past roots and all, to sounds, which drag

my little streams puff & shiver
cover me, my spinner's bird.

"buzzards were drying themselves down there

they leave a place empty I belong to"
early riser, you're all wet & glued to my face

"they leave a miserable bed on the inside"

Dear Goozle, It's Not Mine

You asked what good our songs might do
at this hour. thoughts of good cheer I'm sending
you nonetheless. tease off a few; they're not mine,
though I understand they can be eaten like artichokes.
and we? no views of shadowed mountains here,
but sawdust trails & ample red osiers.
& we do our best to maintain the monolithic samba,
a kind of macho posturing. sometimes that's enough,
fucker. when you wrote *last straw*, I thought
Last Things & what my dictionary says
about casual hairdos & handsome shoes:
"—but they didn't last." I thought this might
be of some importance. with this unseasonable
warmth comes the inevitable meltwater
measuring its way in seeps through
the basement mortar. the hour, dear Goozle,
isn't ours. this hasn't started off well at all.

The Carny Phones from Paradise

Our signals would have been of little use
through the peephole, we agreed. private amusements
reduced to "be very careful." first kiss
in the trauma of the furniture covered with white
sheets, the door left open for air, "hiss." a block
away, a carnival: *tilt-a-whirl, blue streak, devil's teacup...*
"the mattress held all of us cousins over the ash & rust"
what music of summer bounces under
this pumice of stars. "slippage," blowing in our ears
at the top of the world — to the front & rear, lacuna.
we hovered, held fast. dark birds tore past:
the moon returning its borrowed light.

Chess Piece

*

bishop:
the all eyes.
where my hands have gripped, / forms have fallen / as far as I can see.

*

pawn:
foot-soldier, pedal, penniless.
marched into the light for fingering the poorbox, / we who are not
the angels, / but the salts for their pain, / freeze.

*

king:
offspring of the people.
kin:
gene, generate, gonorrhea.
amnesiac kin-sphere flickers / through the light and the dark of me, /
the walking cenotaph.

*

mate:
matador, meat.
check, the king is dead.
we feel for our wife in the dark. / on our nightstand the whiskey /
slowly consumes the ice. / on the buses, the stilled things start upright
            in their seats.

Antigone Sequence

#(audition with Sophocles)

S. I call them scene paintings. you crouch there in the vastly

A. : flyapart.
    and my father?

S. chiseling out the sockets for a closer look

A. : an insuck of sacristy, crowded and icy.
    and I'm his bowgrace?
    I remember
    how you could change us into birds just before we hit
    the earth.

S. continue as if the lines you've memorized
    could be memorized

The Methodists' Rocket's Controlled
Explosion and You

Tried solving it at the church bazaar — salt
Glows from the remnants. Leave-taking,
Purpled with the desire to touch, I do:
Muddy cumin of damp wood in the gym
Alcove; scratchy frou-frou in a muddle
Of fug, would you do me a blurb, right here?
"All these mysterious houses graved out
In bright latex red . . . a humanizing."
A twin, a twin could speak at birth —
There was drinking, singing, some cried. Put this
Someplace private, gunnysack with a glint
Figuring shadows.   Unearthing "hellos,"
Meat pies, primo thrift sales, all good children —
Ten, nine, eight, seven —

Letter from Kabul

dear friend, I have to do with death.
mostly I write from here:

star bright
fever we call daisy cutter,
fifteen thousand pounds of pure sound
caught up in the meter,

sings toward the feverish blades,
and grass eyes blink out
all over. good night to whomever.
ignite.

Field Book

Prickly Pear . . . Opuntia . . . fleshy water-filled jellies and jams.

Mulefat . . . sunflower family . . . scattered teeth on riparian leaves.

Yerba Santa . . . thick, medicinal feeling . . . holy, leathery hands.

California Sagebrush . . . false sage, proclaiming bogus lineage . . .
    nursing Spanish wounds and swellings.

Witch's Hair . . . Dodder . . . parasitic, host seldom killed . . .

Castor Bean . . . poison, atremble with reluctant shade . . . comforts Jonah,
    fresh from the mouth of a great fish, who sulks in a booth
    at the roadside, awaiting the ruin of a city . . .

thinly under

I was afraid how it might dawn again
& to talk nervous, "some nice girl used to

but amazement wouldn't fit inside
ears to the dark wood, we played ruin

hearing long past orange trees & street maps
the flesh as augury & all we swiftly —

pulse. thinly under skin & star
— blue night (put there by) (   )

as if a bird were held

When the Water in the Skin was Gone

Looking for an unmutilated place —
At every periphery lies
Something terribly roadside

: God's footprint —
A hole
Big enough for child-house.

: A quiet that will never
Be silenced —
From an arid language

Driven toward fire

Antigone Sequence

#(on Polynices)

did you see him in the tabloids? my uncle's
soldiers in the picture — o, one hooks my brother's
scalp, wrenches his eyes (still open)
toward the camera. another knuckledeeps
through heart-wound.
it don't learn that in one day.
Headline:
uncle won't bury bad meat.
what else could I do?
I drove out there.
the ground was hard, unbroken.
my sister, part of my body, stayed in the car.
nothing left that was warm to the touch,
I shoveled.

Forcing House

Ironmongers knock about rumors
of lives not hewn
from solitude.

Those whose jars we dust we dream
warm in their amber
floats.

Their pale fingers under-flower,
never bird-spread, but incandesce
the intuited god.

Listless on the surface
of a deafened ear
stirs

the emptiest of horizons.
Something like love

unravels selvages,
tugs at each of our names
where the green lies watchful.

Resolution

Designated floater, I am struck

Silent within the haunted forgettery

The human eye is pages

& pages turned transparent

Lovingly my radio

India-inked China rose in eyeshot, wing on wing

In the buzz between two nearly equal wavelengths, I resist

The move from dissonance to consonance

The appliances are dying, singing their choir

The shudder & glow of wires sustains my milk

the buzz between nearly equal wavelengths

the older I get
the more I'm convinced
memory is purely poetic process
I'm not making this up
at the party   I walked over
to you in the kitchen
when I asked
where do I know you   from
I sort of became   invisible

spring   & you're perfect
light   & everything
sex   (but nothing's new:
radio static
        too many ghosts
)
& I remain
staring
at the animal

small incursions   every word
bird of doubt   bright as jumper cable
on little bits of paper   practice *death*
practice *nobody*
practice *empty sky*

the church marquee reads   *float on*
my agonizingly beautiful
shoes

Antigone Sequence

#(lacuna)

　　　　　[. . .] hole instead of the word [. . .] —
the gods [. . .] have left us
— light switches, shit, suit-coats, [. . .] [. . .] [. . .]
　　　　　yelps of red-tight syllables. [. . . tell-tales.] this is home.
[" . . .] and I'm the [. . . one . . .] who will pour you down its wide throat."

Memnon's Flocks

our violence whirrs   figure of eight
from an early place

through the seed house   Blackwall hitch
empty's generative spread   utter patience

making a new plea   petiole rising
where dew lies scattered   dream into it

over the Phrygian battlefield   a torsion of clover
dawn stutters black spirals   lets out the breath

as it worlds   the body answers

The Off-Scourings of the Hog

If I succumb to hunger   pouring sand
At my sunken hips   a bow, and arrows made from scratch
Already leaching into leaves   poking for small game
Or picking at Jerusalem Crickets behind damp stacks of plywood

To knock at your house of uncertain aspirins
Strike-anywhere   my feeble reprobate lamps
And all these brittle slivers   red with me
And these awkward hard-ons

If I have to ask   what do I know
And who are you   behind this darkling Woolworths
Where the stalking moon fingers us
Through slanted trestle slats

To convince my wracked windows it isn't time
By screaming out of them *it is not time*

Visitation

*

endemic silence of the pear

the moon's ceruse faces
dangle from windows —
[who stumbles?]

its *thou* a territorial song,
[rustling in the wind out there?]

that drip faucet downstairs

— come December it will build a peal of ice

*

[my longed for sky, hinges sprung
peeled down the color wheel
to its raw metal banks
scares the child I was

as any shudder of angel might
(one angel leaned over to kiss goodnight
with glowing cigarette
winter was his favorite light)]

*

flash of cautery

[I think to myself
before the snow, cherries in my mouth

eis > *hieros*, filled with the divine > *oistros*, anything causing madness > *ice*

from this sacristy]

cool

a good moon   begs of children from pillow to pillow
           houseling fingers in their sleep
     does not lessen the horror

a good moon   wanders across fields to steal turnips
           intimate linens of burden
              the starving chew at its fabric

a good moon   chalks the apple & causes the cat to leap
           ravens hang in knots from its horns
              walking stick, straw bag, feathers, down & dirt

a good moon   notes a toppled chair within the ruins
     paints its sound
           toothpaste for thieves

a good moon   leaves itself at the door
     fills zinc basins with velvet & glass
           the dip of paddles bound in white string

a good moon   when it hears what we've done
     tugs at our hands

Acknowledgments

The following poems have previously appeared in these journals.

"When Possible We Try to See": *Pool 3* (2004)
"quiet store," "Chess Piece": *Volt 12* (2006)
"Field Book," "After Marey's First Mechanical Bird": *Forklift, Ohio 14* (2005)
"Antigone Sequence #(at Colonus)," "Antigone Sequence: #(audition with
Sophocles), "Antigone Sequence: #(on Polynices), "Antigone Sequence:
  #(lacuna)": *Volt 9* (2003)
"When the Water in the Skin Was Gone": *Volt 9* (2003)
"early riser," "thinly under": *Perihelion* (2006)
"Letter from Kabul": *Absomaly 1* (2004)

I am forever grateful to my family and friends, my teachers and students.
Thanks to Luigi Ballerini, Brenda Hillman, Ron Koertge, Mark Levine, Anna
Lewis, Cole Swensen, Stephen Yenser, and Dean Young.

I offer particular and profound gratitude to Cal Bedient, Brian "Bean"
Kennedy, and G.C. Waldrep. Thank you, G.C., for the title "The Off-
Scourings of the Hog."

And thank you, Gillian Conoley, for selecting this manuscript as winner of
the Snowbound Chapbook Award.